Physician Executives:
What, Why, How
Second Edition

By George E. Linney Jr., MD, CPE, FACPE, and Barbara J. Linney, MA

American College of Physician Executives
Suite 200
4890 West Kennedy Boulevard
Tampa, Florida 33609
813/287-2000

ISBN: 0-924674-84-9
Library of Congress Card Number: 00-109863

Printed in the United States of America by Hillsboro Printing Company, Tampa, Florida.

Foreword

It is almost eight years since this book's first edition was published. The world of medical management has undergone seismic change in those years. Managed care organizations took center stage, and system integration became an industry byword. Now, both concepts are in a transition period of uncertain outcome.

Although uncertainty continues to define most discussions and debates about the future of our health care delivery system and the competition for medical management positions has intensified greatly over the past eight years, the demand for physicians with superior clinical skills and practical management education and experience has not ebbed. Physician executives are in a growing profession.

What Roger Schenke, Executive Vice President of the American College of Physician Executives, wrote in the foreword to the first edition of the book holds today: "The question most asked of the American College of Physician Executives by health care organizations involves the roles and responsibilities of the medical director. From physicians, those questions nearly always revolve about how to gain entry to the medical management profession.

"Although the College has always responded with the best information available at the time, we have accompanied our advice with caution. In a rapidly evolving health care system, this still new profession is in flux. No two organizations are likely to approach the position with the same set of needs, or constraints. There is no 'recipe' that can be followed without deviation. We are still talking about a 'menu' of possibilities that must be selected from carefully. No medical staff is likely to be persuaded that there is a 'medical director for all seasons.' No organization should labor under a similar illusion.

"In this new College publication, the possibilities are laid out for the reader. Here is the menu that so many organizations seek. What is more, this is a menu with a map. In carefully crafted steps, this book explains why the medical director position is of benefit to both health care organizations and to the medical profession. It shows the range of possibilities within the position. Those 17 possibilities are perhaps the greatest contribution of the book. But it does more. It shows both organizations interested in medical managers and physicians interested in medical management how to achieve a satisfactory match.

"As the medical management profession grows and expands to meet the changing needs of our health care delivery system. This book will undoubtedly require expansion and revision. For the moment, I believe it is the best guide available for all those interested in medical management."

The time for "expansion and revision" arrived this year. The title of the book has been altered slightly to acknowledge the increased stature of the medical manager in the overall health care management picture. More important, those 17 possibilities have been expanded to 22 in six essential categories of medical management—quality management, physician management, liaison functions, conflict resolution, upper management and governance, and cost management. We believe that the new line-up of possibilities recognizes the physician executive's essential purpose in the management of health organizations—to bring clinical experience and management know-how to bear on bridging the gap between the goals of business success and clinical excellence.

Wesley Curry
Managing Editor, Book Publishing
American College of Physician Executives
October 2000

About the Authors

George E. Linney Jr., MD, CPE, FACPE, is in charge of physician executive recruitment for Tyler & Company, a search firm in Atlanta, Georgia. In addition to his work with Tyler & Company, he is a management consultant, providing strategic planning, leadership development, and management training services to hospitals, medical groups, and managed care organizations.

Prior to establishing his consulting firm, he was Medical Director, EQUICOR of Virginia. He previously was Medical Director, CIGNA Healthplan of Orlando, Florida. Before joining CIGNA in 1983, he had been a pediatrician for 11 years with the Nalle Clinic, Charlotte, North Carolina, where he served in a number of management positions, including Secretary, Treasurer, and Chairman of the Finance Committee.

Dr. Linney received his bachelor's degree from Furman University, Greenville, South Carolina, and his medical degree from the Medical College of Georgia, Augusta. He served his internship and residency in pediatrics at the University of Virginia Medical Center. He is a Diplomate of the American Board of Pediatrics.

Dr. Linney is a co-presenter in the Career Choices program of the American College of Pysician Executives and a teaching fellow for the Certified Physician Executive Tutorial.

Dr. Linney is a Past President of the American College of Physician Executives and served on its Board of Directors for five years. He has been a Delegate to the American Group Practice Association and has served on its Board of Trustees. He is a Fellow of the American College of Physician Executives and is a Certified Physician Executive.

Barbara J. Linney, MA, is Vice President of Career Development for the American College of Physician Executives. She is known for her work in career counseling, management development, and communications training. Barbara's background includes one-on-one counseling, seminar presentations, published articles, and college-level teaching. She is author of the book, *Hope for the Future, A Career Development Guide for Physician Executives.*

Barbara is a graduate of the University of Richmond in Virginia; earned her master's degree at the University of North Carolina-Charlotte; and has completed the coursework for her doctorate at the University of South Florida in Tampa.

Barbara is a co-presenter in the Career Choices program of the American College of Physician Executives and one of the faculty for the Certified Physician Executive Tutorial. She helps develop educational programs, finds new faculty, and oversees onsite programs at ACPE.

College members have heard her speak on topics such as Improving Interpersonal Communications, Conflict Management, Delivering Effective Presentations, Conducting Effective Meetings, and Writing for the Physician Executive.

Contents

Chapter One

An Overview of the Physician Executive's Roles and Responsibilities

This monograph was written to answer questions posed by physicians who are interested in management and by organizations that think they may want to hire physician executives.

Physicians in management have many titles. Medical director is the most frequently used title in group practices and managed care organizations. Vice president of medical affairs is the equivalent position in a hospital. Physician executive is a broader term covering chief executive officers, chief operating officers, medical directors, VPMAs, and all other physicians who are involved in running the business end of medicine as well as the clinical end. We will use the terms physician executive, medical director or physician manager interchangeably. This is to give some variety as you read and to remind you that several different titles are used for those who have stepped over into management territory.

In this chapter, we will describe the functions that physician executives have performed in several organizations. Perhaps no one person would do them all, and your medical director may think of other jobs that need to be done. We'll list the major tasks and then discuss how they are carried out in hospitals, group practices, and managed care organizations. Not every type of organization will be concerned with each of the tasks.

Practicing clinicians are exposed to management in a variety of ways. Some serve on committees and get more and more interested in the workings of the organization. Some are asked by the organization to take on administrative tasks because they are well liked by other physicians. Others have heard that some physicians do management activities, and they are curious about what that means. At some point, they ask, What do medical directors do? What do you have to do to become a medical director?

Organizations that have gotten big enough that volunteer physician manager positions no longer meet their needs often consider having a paid physician manager. They ask, How do you set up the position and give the medical director the proper authority, power, and influence? How can you convince a medical staff that feels threatened by the idea of having a medical director that it needs one?

The physician executive role has been in existence for many years. It expanded dramatically in the '70s and '80s as health care became more organized. As changes in health care have increased in both number and intensity, the need has increased for physicians well versed in management skills to oversee utilization review, quality assurance, physician performance, and other aspects of the direct delivery of patient care. In the '90s, physician executives were asked to give increased attention to cost management and allocation of resources.

Physicians generally do not like to be told what to do, but they will tolerate it from another physician who knows the technical skills of medicine and the peculiar demands of the job. Physicians tend to discount lay managers and dismiss their concerns with the thought, "They know nothing about medicine and taking care of patients." The physician executive's role has grown in importance as the cost crisis continues to dominate health care. Increasingly"...physician executives are involved in administration for proactive reasons, such as having a broad impact on health care delivery, improving the quality of patient care, and the enjoyment of managerial challenges, rather than for the historic reasons of 'someone has to do it' and dissatisfaction with patient care."[1]

What Do Physician Executives Do?

The functions that constitute the shopping list for physician executive responsibilities are shown in the figure on page 3. As mentioned earlier, it is rare that all of these responsibilities would be assigned to any single physician executive. Also, it is likely that some in an individual organization will desire to assign a task that is not included in the list. Our goal in compiling the list was to provide an appropriate beginning point for a physician executive job description. The details of our list follow.

Quality Management

■ *Oversee quality assurance,* or whatever its trendy initials are at the time you read this book. Direction of quality assurance activities is very important in all three of the major sectors. Nurses, medical records librarians, and clerical employees do the day-to-day work of assessing quality of care and then trying to set up systems that will improve it where needed. The physician executive oversees the process. An example of improving quality would be to look at the way in which patients with diabetes are being monitored on an outpatient basis. If you find that some primary care physicians are not monitoring these patients according to the standards of the appropriate national specialty organizations, you would provide all the practitioners who are caring for diabetics with those standards for outpatient monitoring. Then you would reassess the situation in 6-12 months to see that it had improved. Quality assurance lets physicians and the hospital know that they are doing a good job as well as pointing out areas that need improvement.

Another pressing reason to improve quality of care is to satisfy government regulators and any organizations that conduct site visits to assess care, such as the Joint Commission on Accreditation of Healthcare Organizations (JCAHO) and

Basic Roles and Responsibilities of Physician Executives in Hospitals, Group Practices, and Managed Care Organizations

1. Quality Management
- Oversee quality assurance.
- Direct utilization review.
- Ensure compliance with the mission statement, corporate policies, and by-laws.
- Ensure that medical staff efforts meet or exceed standards of the various accrediting and approving bodies.
- Develop clinical guidelines and critical pathways that can be used for outcomes management.
- Oversee all aspects of compliance involving patient care.
- Spearhead the effort for outstanding patient and customer service.

2. Physician Management
- Recruit physicians.
- Evaluate physician performance.
- Manage physician performance.
- Manage physicians who are disruptive or impaired.
- Oversee credentialing and privileging of physicians.
- Develop provider relations.
- Develop staffing plans.

3. Liaison Functions
- Serve as liaison between administration and medical staff.
- Represent the organization to outside groups that interact with his/her organization.

4. Conflict Resolution
- Resolve grievances.
- Mediate professional disputes and interdepartmental problems.

5. Upper Management and Governance
- Serve on the board of directors.
- Participate in strategic planning.

6. Cost Management
- Prepare the expense budget for the medical department.
- Be responsible for medical cost containment and allocation or resources.

the National Committee for Quality Assurance (NCQA). Hospitals and group practices need to have a good quality assurance and quality improvement program in order to satisfy all third-party payers and employers with which they contract. Also, medical quality management is important in all three major sectors as a marketing and promotions tool. For example:

— A group practice can say it is accredited by JCAHO or NCQA.

— A hospital making a sales presentation to a managed care organization or to a large employer can say it has the lowest nosocomial infection rate in the geographic area.

■ *Direct utilization review.* Utilization review is prospective, concurrent, or retrospective assessment of how all medical resources are being used to care for patients. This function is most important in an managed care organization, but it is also important in a hospital setting and a physician organization.

In a managed care organization, a staff of clerical employees and nurses gathers and tracks information first about expensive health care items, such as hospital admissions and length of stay for those admissions, necessity for surgery, and necessity for continued care in skilled nursing facilities or for home care. Staff members also look at requests by physicians for significant tests, such as MRls; surgical procedures; and referrals to specialists. The medical director and the staff deal with requests for all the above items and decide:

— Whether they are medically necessary.

— Whether they are benefits covered in the person's insurance benefits package.

— Whether less expensive alternatives to the care that is proposed by the physician should be considered.

Happily for physicians and their support staff, the intensity of oversight by managed care organizations is lessening.

In a managed care organization, or in a group practice that also has a managed care component, decision making about less expensive alternatives is extremely important, because that process enables the managed care organization or component to control and monitor the outlay of premium dollars. There is a limit to the amount of money that can be spent. Realistically, the limit is based on the amount of money that is gathered through premiums. Deficit spending gets you in trouble quickly.

In a hospital, utilization review is a little bit different, because the hospital is not paying out dollars for care, but it does have to be quite responsible to Medicare and to all third-party payers, so a staff of nurses and other record keepers is necessary. This activity should be overseen by the hospital medical director.

■ *Ensure compliance with the corporate mission statement, policies, and by-laws.* The medical director needs to think about the organization's mission statement and keep reminding the organization of it. "Are we doing what we said we were going to do when we wrote the mission statement at the retreat two years ago?" Everyone gets excited when a mission statement is developed, but then they go back and get busy with their clinical practices or management tasks. The medical director needs to be the one who doesn't forget and who keeps thinking about ways to carry it out.

The corporate policies and by-laws are written documents that must be adhered to in order to protect all parties working in the organization and all customers that the organization serves. The medical director should be familiar with them and should remind people of their contents when necessary.

■ *Ensure that medical staff efforts meet or exceed standards of the various accrediting and approving bodies.* The medical director is responsible for ensuring that the organization is prepared for all audits or accreditation visits by any federal or state organizations that are responsible for accreditation as well as by organizations such as JCAHO and NCQA. Preparation for these audits is a continual process, and, although staff-level people can be responsible for the nuts and bolts and the paperwork, the medical director must see to it that the whole process comes together in a timely fashion. If everyone works together in the areas of quality assurance, risk management, professional credentialing, and adherence to by-laws and policies, the actual site visits will be less of a headache for everyone involved.

■ *Develop clinical guidelines and critical pathways that can be used for outcomes management.* It is the responsibility of the medical director in any organization to see that clinicians and various specialty departments work together to develop appropriate guidelines for inpatient and outpatient care. The physician executive should not be handing out guidelines but should be enabling physicians in each specialty to develop guidelines utilizing national experience, specialty organization standards, and their own local experience. This should provide patient care at the best cost and result in the best long-term outcomes.

■ *Oversee all aspects of compliance involving patient care.* In the past five years, compliance has become one of the buzz words in health care management. An increasing number of regulatory bodies and watch-dog organizations have made compliance a daily concern for all payers and providers. There are so many regulations to keep up with that most hospitals and delivery systems of any size at all have found it necessary to have compliance officers. In some organizations, this responsibility falls to the chief medical officer, but, at the least, the physician executive should be responsible for all compliance issues involving patient care.

■ *Spearhead the effort for outstanding patient and customer service.* The chief medical officer and the chief executive officer of any provider or payer organization must be the "flag wavers" for outstanding patient and customer service. Superior service will be the differentiator in this new decade. Customers, whoever they are, will assume that quality of care is a given and that the price offered is the best price they can expect for a given service.

It is the duty of top executives to talk about superior service daily and to model it consistently to their employees as they serve their various customers in the work place.

Physician Management

■ *Recruit physicians.* In a group practice, the medical director recruits physicians who will work for the organization and become partners or shareholders. It is typically the responsibility of the medical director in a group practice to direct all the functions that are related to recruitment. Planning for recruitment should occur at least a year before the time you need a physician. It should take place even earlier if you have needs in hard-to-obtain specialties.

Someone on the medical director's staff does the clerical work involved in the recruitment process. An outside firm or an internal recruiter may get the process started, but the medical director is an integral part of the process. The task requires that one be organized and plan ahead, but it also is a sales job. It's helpful if the medical director enjoys this kind of activity, because it involves many communication skills—telephone interviews, face-to-face interviews, socializing, and listening (an important part of the sales process).

To recruit physicians, the medical director must first have a clear idea of what the group wants—for example, a general internist who subspecializes in geriatrics. Then the search begins, using internal recruiters, telephone calls, advertisements in journals, recruiting letters, and/or search firms to identify interested candidates. Physicians who are interested will send in resumes or curricula vitae. The medical director will screen the curricula vitae, check references, and talk to the candidates on the phone before deciding which ones to invite for face-to-face interviews with other members of the group. The medical director will be responsible for scheduling the candidate's visits; working out lodging; developing a general schedule for formal interviews with the candidates; and planning tours of the facility, hospitals, and city. He or she will also coordinate social events so the physician and spouse can meet other doctors and spouses. No position should be offered to a physician unless his or her spouse has visited at least once and the physician has visited at least twice.

The medical director also helps the candidate and the organization decide if a good match can be made. Will the personalities mesh and get along? Can they compensate for each other's weaknesses? Will they want to? Do they have similar values, or can each party respect the dissimilarities? This is a complex activity and is often given little attention. In a dynamic group practice, there probably will be significant recruitment needs each year, so this may be one of the most important functions that the group practice medical director provides.

The recruitment function in staff-model managed care organizations is very similar to that in group practices. In independent physician association (IPA) models, it is very different, because you are not recruiting associates or partners. You are asking physicians to participate in the IPA —physicians who will agree to contract with the managed care organization to take care of its members. The medical director meets with physicians in all sorts of private practice settings to sell them on the merits of joining forces with the managed care organization and eventually must get them to sign contracts. In stronger IPAs, the medical director clearly directs this function and is personally involved in the recruitment activities on a daily basis.

In many IPAs, the physician recruitment function is carried out by nonmedical staff. This is not a good idea, because some physicians may be signed on who, for various reasons, will become problems to the managed care organization and its members as time goes on. Nonmedical employees do not have a good way of knowing if they are signing high-quality physicians. They have to rely on the credentialing process, which has limited usefulness in this regard. The medical director can more easily talk to other physicians in the community to find out who the better doctors are. He or she can also ask pointed questions to determine the physician's skills and practice habits.

The recruitment of doctors in hospitals is very different from that in groups and managed care organizations, but the medical director still may play a vital role in recruiting private practicing physicians to the hospital medical staff. This may sometimes involve urging certain types of specialists or primary care physicians to switch primary allegiance from another hospital to the medical director's hospital. In other cases, it may be a matter of recruiting physicians from outside the community to move to that city and practice at that hospital. In a hospital with special needs, the recruitment function could be very significant. In a hospital with a relatively stable medical staff and plenty of specialists in all the important areas, recruitment might be a very insignificant responsibility.

■ *Evaluate physician performance.* In a group practice, evaluation of physician performance is absolutely necessary, but, if the group is large, the medical director cannot do all of the evaluations. He or she should evaluate no more than five or six people. Then the people who report to him or her should have five or six people to evaluate and so on down until everyone is assigned an evaluator. The department chairs are an integral part of this evaluation hierarchy. However, it would be important for the medical director's office to see that the whole process is carried out in an appropriate and timely fashion. This means reminding the various evaluators to schedule face-to-face evaluations in the appropriate time frame, giving each physician a self-evaluation form (designed by the organization) to review and possibly to fill out prior to the meeting with the evaluator. The reviewer would write an evaluation of the meeting to be given to the physician and put in his or her file. It would be the medical director's responsibility to review all these written evaluation summaries after the individual meetings have occurred.

In addition, the medical director, along with an evaluation committee, makes sure that the group has a good system for periodic performance evaluations and that the written form is appropriate and useful. The medical director would also work with department chairs to be sure that the loop is completed in cases where the physician is given constructive criticism, with a timetable for improvement and reevaluation. Part of the feedback for each clinician should address whether he or she is meeting group and national norms in his or her specialty. The physician manager needs skills and sensitivity in giving feedback so that the physician can understand what he or she is doing wrong and then work on a plan for how he or she can improve. The evaluation process must include some sort of reward and penalty system, which usually means you receive a monetary award if things are going well and you don't if your performance is not up to the organization's standards.

Most people would agree that performance evaluations should be done on all physicians in a group practice at least annually. Probably new physicians should have a formal evaluation within 90 days of the time they joined the organization and possibly one more time before the annual review.

In staff model HMOs, the process would be very similar to that in group practices. In IPA models, the only evaluation that is usually done is to periodically check and track different types of utilization by the members of the IPA. If significant complaints from members are directed at a physician, they can also be used as part of the evaluation. However, in a large IPA, if the physician has reasonable utilization and does not have significant member complaints, it's usually difficult to do much of a formal evaluation, especially if the physician's office does not do a large volume of care for the HMO.

In most hospitals in which members of the medical staff are independent private practitioners, it is very difficult to do much formal evaluation. However, it has become increasingly common to give members of the medical staff feedback regarding their individual lengths of stay and their utilization of resources as compared to other members of their department. Sometimes, a formal evaluation process is carried out on new members of the medical staff within a year after they begin their associations. The hospital medical director oversees the process, but the department chair usually does the evaluation.

■ *Manage physician performance.* The medical director in a group practice or a staff-model managed care organization will be responsible for keeping up with physician productivity, cost-effective practice, and patient satisfaction, as well as other issues. Some of these activities will be monitored on a monthly basis, and the medical director will review that information and pass it down the chain of command to division heads or department chairs so that those people can, in turn, give regular feedback to their colleagues. "A model to effectively influence behavior includes setting clear expectations, measuring and monitoring performance, providing feedback, and rewarding and recognizing improvement."[2] These activities are related to the periodic formal evaluations but are done on a more frequent basis so that quick fixes and changes can be made.

At times, the medical director will need to confront physicians about poor clinical performance or poor interpersonal behavior. Chapter 3 gives suggestions for how to do this.

■ *Manage physicians who are disruptive or impaired.** An experienced group practice administrator has successfully used the following methods: Talk with the suspected impaired physician in a nonjudgmental way, in a calm, firm voice describing what is perceived to be the problem. Don't challenge the physician if he or she denies there is a problem or explains why people might erroneously perceive that there is a problem. Just state the facts as perceived and develop with this physician ways to resolve the perceived problems. Some examples of this approach follow:

— *Physician who is chronically late completing medical records.* The medical director or department chair should confront the physician with the facts and remind him or her of the organization's standards as established in the by-laws. The physician should be reminded that he or she must comply with the standards, and the medical director may ask if there is a way that the organization can help the physician with compliance—for example, by providing extra clerical help. Then the medical director and the physician must agree on a time table for correcting the problem. The medical director should state that he or she will check on the status of the physician's medical records in a certain period(e.g., 30 or 60 days). If the problem has been corrected, no further action will be taken. If the problem has not been resolved, punitive measures, such as temporary loss of privileges or withholding of pay, will be instituted.

— *Suspected alcoholic physician.* Say to the physician, "People say they smell alcohol on your breath, and they are concerned you are drinking during working hours." The physician usually denies this and provides various explanations: "I use a strong aftershave." "It must be my mouth wash." Do not challenge these explanations, but indicate that the physician needs to make some changes so that perceptions will change. At the second meeting, if one is needed and it most likely will be, restate the facts. Propose a contract with the physician to draw a blood alcohol level next time a problem is perceived. The physician will generally agree to this since, in his or her opinion, he or she has nothing to fear. When a problem is evident again, draw a blood alcohol as agreed. This is done in the presence of another physician so there can be no question about the procedure's being done properly or about the physician's agreeing voluntarily to have the blood alcohol done. If the blood alcohol is high, as anticipated, the physician is advised to get treatment or leave the organization. Many organizations maintain the physician's income and pay for the treatment if the physician is a long-term member of the organization. After the physician returns from treatment, the blood alcohol is monitored periodically. The physician is advised that, if there is a relapse, he or she must leave the organization.

---

* *The authors wish to thank John W. Pollard, MD, MBA, CPE, FACPE, former Chief Executive Officer, Carle Clinic Association, Urbana, Ill., for major contributions to this section on dealing with the impaired physician.*

— *Physician having an affair with an employee of the clinic.* Basically, the same approach used for the alcoholic physician is taken, describing to the physician people's perceptions. It is important to emphasize that no one knows whether or not the perceptions are true, but, whether they are true or not, they need to change. Nearly always, the physician changes his or her behavior, either ending the affair or at least separating it from the work environment.

— *Physician with declining abilities or dementia.* Advise the physician that colleagues believe he or she is no longer as capable as necessary and that he or she must stop practicing medicine. How soon this must happen depends on the severity of the decline in skills. The incentives to encourage compliance with the suggestions are, in order of use: 1) you may hurt a patient; 2) you may damage your reputation and the reputation of the organization; 3) you are risking a bad malpractice suit; and 4) formal action will be taken to limit your privileges and/or remove you from the staff. By step three, concurrence about how to proceed is usually reached. Sometimes, a reference to number four is needed to achieve agreement.

■ ***Oversee credentialing and privileging of physicians.*** This function is important in all three of the major sectors and has increased in importance as regulatory bodies have demanded more specific credentialing as well as accrediting of organizations. It has become increasingly important for organizations in which physicians work to prove to prospective users of services that their physicians are of high quality. Much of the credentialing activity involves just collecting the various pieces of paper that attest that the physician has been to medical school, has had postgraduate training, is board certified, and does not have any significant malpractice history (or, if there is history of malpractice, the results can be explained to everyone's satisfaction and be accepted by the organization where he or she is going to work).

Other common concerns to be addressed are verification that the physician has the appropriate malpractice coverage, that he or she has no history of impairment (or that he or she is acceptably recovering from impairment), and that he or she has no criminal history.

Most credentials collecting is cut and dried and can be done by support staff. However, it is the function of the medical director to make judgments and recommendations in any of the gray or questionable areas. It is also important that the organization do credentialing in such a way that it is consistent with its bylaws and in a way that will not make it liable for civil actions brought by physicians who are not accepted on the staff because of failing the credentialing process.

Privileging of physicians is allied with the credentialing effort but is more specific. It entails verifying that the physician is appropriately trained to do whatever technical procedures that he or she is asking permission to do. The medical director decides what procedures a physician can do on the basis of information given on the privileging application. Finally, it should be the responsibility of the medical director and the organization to make the credentialing process as easy as possible for every physician on the staff. Currently practicing physicians have to provide credentialing information to numerous organizations: hospitals, IPAs, payer organizations, etc. This requires an inordinate amount of time from the physician and his or her support staff. Anything that can be done to make the process simpler would be appreciated by the physician.

■ *Develop provider relations.* Managed care organizations are most concerned with developing provider relations. The medical director, with the help of staff in the department of provider relations, should be responsible for contracting with physicians, hospitals, and all other agencies or businesses that will provide any type of medical care to members. The relationship between the managed care organization and the various providers must be satisfactory to both parties and must be tended to on a daily basis. The managed care organization will usually have a standard for how many regular telephone calls and how many face-to-face calls are made to each provider. The face-to-face visits may range in frequency from once a year to once a quarter. Routine telephone contact frequency might range from once a quarter to once a month.

The relationships must also be satisfactory to the individuals who will receive health care through the managed care organization and to the corporations and businesses that are paying for that care. The receiver of the care, the deliverer of the care, and the payer of that care are all customers. Lack of regular attention to those relationships will severely affect member satisfaction, utilization of resources, and cost containment, and can certainly affect the quality of care delivered to members. Once contracts have been established, the medical director and the provider relations staff maintain and update them. The process includes being sure on an ongoing basis that the provider is satisfied with the terms of the contract.

The medical director and the provider relations staff should also determine the number of providers available to the managed care organization. For example, what will be the number of hospitals, of primary care physicians, of specialists, of contracted laboratories, of skilled nursing facilities, and of physical therapy providers available in a given service area. The number needed in each case is based on the number of members, the geographic distribution of those members, the demands of corporate clients, and the demands of individuals.

The medical director should work with the marketing and sales department and the customer relations department to provide adequate access to medical services for members. However, it is important to remember that those two departments will always be asking for more providers, and it is the job of the medical director to negotiate for an appropriate balance. Corporate clients and individual members will perceive that more providers available to them is more satisfactory; however, utilization control, cost containment, and quality assurance can be managed much better with fewer rather than more providers.

The medical director should be sure that the provider relations staff visits each contracted provider an appropriate number of times per year and that these visits occur regularly and not just when problems and grievances arise. Providers who do a lot of business with the managed care organization should probably be visited three or four times a year, whereas those who do less business can be handled with one or two visits per year.

Finally, the medical director should be directly involved with significant grievances that the managed care organization has toward a provider or vice versa, especially if the grievances involve quality of care or service to patients.

■ *Develop staffing plans.* Developing staffing plans involves deciding, for example, how many pediatricians or utilization review nurses are needed. The medical director should develop the staffing plan for anyone who reports directly to him or her or who reports to his or her direct subordinates. It makes no sense at all for staffing plans to be given to a medical director by people higher than the medical director or people not involved in his or her day-to-day operations. Certainly guidelines for those plans can and should be given to the medical director, but the specifics of the plan should be worked out by the person who runs that department.

Usually, there are general industrial guidelines for organizations such as staff-model managed care organizations and, to a lesser extent, IPAs. If the managed care organization is part of a large national organization, there are organization-specific guidelines. If there are no guidelines, it should be the responsibility of the medical director to develop a staffing plan that is consistent with the general and specific functions that his or her department must perform and that are also in line with health industry guidelines and budget constraints. The staffing plan should be generated first, and the staffing budget should be developed from it, rather than vice versa.

Liaison Functions

■ *Serve as liaison.* A major function for physician executives in managed care organizations, group practices, and hospitals is to serve as liaison between physicians and administrative personnel. Traditionally, administrators in any of the three major sectors and practicing physicians have had a hard time understanding each other. They have different agendas, values, and priorities. Often, they don't trust each other. They even have different vocabularies. Physician executives have the advantage of understanding something about both sides. They grew up in the physician culture, and, even though the administrative camp is newer to them, they can gradually learn the values, priorities, and vocabularies in that arena. More and more, they will also benefit from having some of the same formal training and education that the administrators have, so that can be the link between the two camps. They can explain issues to each party and be interpreters. Richard Roodman, CEO of Valley Medical Center, Renton, Washington, puts it this way: "The medical director speaks the language of the medical staff and has the credibility a lay person can't have....The director functions as a 'trust builder' where anxiety and paranoia are rampant."[3]

If this task is done well, it may be the one that is the most valuable to the organization. "Having a physician skilled in medical administration reassures the medical staff that administration is genuinely concerned about the unique demands physicians face in the practice of their profession. At the same time, the hospital's chief administrative officials need assurances that complex policy questions that directly affect clinical issues are being handled by a competent, full-time manager who is knowledgeable about medical procedures and also is aware of modern management techniques."[4]

■ *Represent the organization to outside groups that interact with his or her organization.* Often, the physician executive is called on to be a liaison with outside organizations. This includes community organizations with which the hospital, managed care organization, or group practice deals, such as employer coalitions, county medical societies, hospitals with which the group practice or managed care organization does business, and companies or employee groups with which the organization does or would like to do business. Whenever there is a significant issue about health care, any of those types of organizations in the community want to hear from "the doctor," not just the administrator, a salesperson, or a marketing person. If the organization is sensitive to its various outside constituencies, the physician executive needs to be out in the community regularly, and not just hearing or reading reports of what is going on from second- or third-hand sources.

Conflict Resolution

■ *Resolve grievances.* If grievances come from patients and are directed toward physicians for whom the medical director is responsible, it is imperative that the medical director be directly responsible for resolving them. Sometimes, the medical director may simply make the doctor aware of a patient's dissatisfaction and ask him or her to talk with the patient by telephone or write to the patient if a more formal response is necessary. Most of the time, it is better if the physician responds to the complaint rather than having the medical director handle the apology directly. This usually results in greater patient satisfaction and also is helpful in educating the physician and reducing the chances that the problem will recur.

If the patient complaint is not directed at physician care or behavior but rather at some business policy of the organization or at a nurse or some other type of employee, it is probably better for the medical director to pass the handling of the grievance to the appropriate manager in the organization.

Similarly, the medical director should handle complaints and grievances from a physician. These would be very common in an IPA-type managed care organization. For example, the physician may have a complaint concerning what he or she was paid for a procedure. The medical director should handle such a complaint unless it is mainly a complaint involving business policies, such as the timeliness of a claim payment or the handling of a claim. In summary, it should always be the medical director's responsibility to recognize who the organization's customers are and to respond to their complaints in a timely fashion, even if they cannot be satisfied. The customers can be patients, physicians, other providers, or employers.

- *Mediate professional disputes and interdepartmental problems.* It is the responsibility of the medical director to mediate professional disputes and interdepartmental problems. The medical director is a liaison person or interface agent and will have to use his or her best negotiating and mediating skills to handle disputes between two physicians of the same or different specialties. These disputes are likely to involve finances or power, but may occasionally be over quality of medical care concerns. It will be the duty of the medical director to collect the facts, facilitate effective communication between the disputing parties, and occasionally render a final decision when the two parties cannot work out a solution themselves. The hardest thing for the medical director to do will be to keep his or her personal feelings about the issue or the opponents in the background.

The same negotiating and mediating skills will be required for interdepartmental problems. These could be disputes between a clinical department and medical records, between surgeons and operating room nurses, or between emergency department physicians and cardiologists.

Upper Management and Governance

- *Serve on the board of directors.* In group practices, it would be absolutely necessary for the medical director to serve on the board of directors, although it might be quite common for him or her not to have a vote. Whether the medical director does or does not have formal voting power doesn't matter, because the people who have the most knowledge about what's going on usually have the most power in a board meeting, whether that is the medical director, the senior administrator of the group, or anyone else. It would also be appropriate for the medical director of a managed care organization to serve on the board; however, boards of managed care organizations vary greatly. Sometimes they only include high-level executives at the national level in the organization. At the other extreme, the board in a local managed care organization may be made up primarily of members rather than providers of services or executives of the managed care organization. Even in that case, it would be appropriate for the medical director to participate in meetings. Likewise in a hospital setting, the medical director or vice president of medical affairs should certainly attend board meetings whether he or she has a vote or not.

The medical director from time to time will assume responsibility for special projects as assigned by the board of directors—for example, direct a specific quality assurance study in response to a consumer concern or complaint.

- *Participate in strategic planning.* In an organization in which the medical director is a high-level executive, he or she should probably be responsible for or at least play an integral part in the ongoing process of strategic planning. In an organization that either delivers or manages patient care, the medical director should be the number two ranking officer, second only to the chief executive officer. Many management experts believe that the biggest responsibility of the highest level executives should be strategic planning. Strategic planning involves both short- and long-range planning, and it must be an ongoing process rather than something that occurs only at periodic board meetings or retreats. Strategic planning should precede the program planning and the budget planning processes. Furthermore, if the medical director is to be an effective leader in the planning processes, it is important that he or she have formal education as well as practical on-the-job training in strategic planning. He or she could watch the process, assist someone with the planning, and finally be fully in charge of the process.

Cost Management

■ *Prepare the expense budget for the medical department.* If the medical director is to have any significant authority at all, he or she must be responsible for preparing the budget on a periodic basis. Traditionally, companies prepare budgets annually, but some companies now revise them semiannually or quarterly. Usually, the nuts and bolts of budget preparation can be delegated to subordinates, but the medical director should always have final approval of the proposed budget for his or her department that will then be coordinated with budgets of other departments in the organization. In the worst scenario, the medical director is handed a budget for his or her department that was developed by others and is still given the responsibility to operate within the constraints of the budget. A surprising number of health care organizations still operate this way.

■ *Be responsible for medical cost containment and allocation of resources.* Near the end of the previous decade, hospital CEOs and boards wisely realized that the medical director must have direct responsibility for managing costs related to patient care in the institution. Large multispecialty groups and other more formal physician organizations have come to this realization also. This increased responsibility for the medical director has been good not only for the organizations, but also for the physician executive, as it has provided him or her the opportunity to demonstrate expertise in financial management as well as traditional medical management.

No one person would do all of the 22 tasks above. The list was generated by reading many job descriptions, which vary tremendously from organization to organization. Ideally, an organization will determine what problems it is having and then hire a medical director who can help it solve them.

Physician Executive Role to Expand

Russ Coile,[5] a futurist, and others[6,7] predict some new roles and responsibilities for physician executives as well as some changes in the familiar job. These emerging opportunities promise to greatly expand the career ladder for physician executives, and, as attested to in the following descriptions, bring them to positions of increased authority and influence. Physicians aspiring to leadership roles in organizations will keep their options open.

"Don't get comfortable with your job description. Tomorrow's physician executives will take on expanding sets of career opportunities and leadership roles including:

"**Chief executive officer**—Large hospitals and health systems are searching for high-trust physician executives with business skills and demonstrated leadership abilities....These physician CEOs will walk a tightrope between the patients' first demands of their professional colleagues and board requirements for economic performance. Those who can get the mix right will be among the vanguard of health care CEOs in the next decade."[5] Coile reports that he has seen more chief medical officers become CEOs since his earlier article.[8]

"'Current wisdom' predicts that, within ten years, most health care organizations of any size will have a physician as CEO. The two main reasons are: (1) if the business of health care is health care, the person at the top should understand the core competencies. (2) It is easier to teach a clinician business principles than to teach a business person about health sciences. (3) From a cost accounting viewpoint, the most critical persons in the health care environment are physicians. They initiate almost all of the significant variable expenditures. (4) Understanding physician culture and relating to that constituency are critical to the future success of the community health enterprise."[6]

"**Chief operations officer**—The COO will drive the organization's core business—patient care—but will also oversee many other clinical and administrative support functions. A critical challenge will be developing a close working relationship with nursing executives who directly manage patient care services. Nursing may resent not having an RN in the chief operating officer position."[5]

"**Chief medical officer**—The CMO is a diplomat, first and foremost, providing liaison and representation between the provider organizations and the community's physicians and medical groups....The CMO will be engaged in endless negotiations over some of the most sensitive issues that could divide hospitals and their physicians....CMO job descriptions will be broad and vague, at least in the near future."[5]

"**Chief technology officer**—This 'senior scientist" position will be based in large health systems, academic medical centers, pharmaceutical manufacturers, and other health industry suppliers....Their primary role will be to scan the technology horizon for promising R & D that could enhance their organization's clinical services or provide an opportunity for product development."[5] Coile has subsequently indicted that guiding organizational investments in genomics and biotechnology will be an important part of this position's responsibilities.[8]

"**Vice president for quality**—A strong research orientation and analytic skills are prerequisites for this position. Some VPs will be epidemiologists.....They will lead quality improvement and clinical pathway initiatives and conduct studies of their organizations' outcome and cost data."[5]

"**Managed care medical director**—Managed care medical directors will work on the plan side for HMOs, insurance companies, preferred provider organizations, as well as on the provider side for provider-sponsored managed care organizations....Their primary role as utilization manager will be broadened to include more analysis of variations in medical care and outcomes within their enrolled population, applying sophisticated techniques of data analysis to 'mine' their data warehouses for opportunities for quality and cost improvement."[5]

"**Medical division vice president/MSO executive**—Physician executives will manage the growing number of provider-owned physician practices among the nation's 20,000 medical groups....This is an expanding field that will reward physician executives who can successfully generate a bottom-line from these groups."[5]

"**Service-line manager**—Today's clinical program medical directors will be the service-line managers of tomorrow. These physician executives will combine clinical expertise with marketing and business management skills."[5]

The preceding list of expanded job titles is by no means exhaustive. The dramatically changing structure of the health care delivery system and its constituent parts ensures that new functions ideally suited to the special expertise of physician executives will continue to arise. This tendency will be abetted by the equally dramatic rise in new technologies and in the adaptation of existing technologies to medicine and the health care field.

Boruch says that physician executives must attend to what he calls "practicalities." "Many practitioners have already garnered advanced clinical training, formal business education, and multiple health-oriented degrees. More will and should do so. Two aspects of health care that seem destined for explosive growth in the near future are telemedicine and biotechnology. To enhance our individual and collective marketability even further, it would seem wise to enrich our knowledge in these two areas...."[7]

Chapter Two

How to Set up the Position of Physician Executive

Seek General Agreement

To begin, there needs to be general agreement on why the organization needs a physician executive. The physicians and administration need a physician executive who can live in both camps and can understand and explain the priorities and values of each group to the other. A hospital or any other provider or payer organization needs one or more physicians who have the time, the interest, and the expertise to do quality management, credentialing, accreditation preparation, medical staff conflict resolution, and all the management functions that only a physician executive can do. Sometimes, physicians resist having these functions done by someone they perceive as a boss. Administrators are sometimes threatened by physician executives invading their management territory, especially a position that is going to add considerably to the salary budget. If the medical director can talk to both of these groups, he or she can help all of them feel less threatened and thus better able to communicate.

Sometimes these positions have been set up for the wrong reasons. For example, administrators might say, "We need somebody to get the doctors in line or bring the doctors around to our way of thinking." Physicians might want the medical director to do things that the full-time clinicians don't want to do or don't have the time to do. While the medical director will do some of those tasks, taking that attitude to the extreme could be bad. Physicians can't just give all of the quality assurance and utilization review functions to the medical director. If they do, physicians could abdicate leadership and be totally uninvolved. It becomes an organization that belongs to administration rather than to the doctors. Some large organizations have folded because the doctors did not know what was going on. However, in most organizations there are important functions that physicians in volunteer positions as committee chairs or board members say that they are doing, but they may not be doing them well. Perhaps they don't know how to do the tasks, don't have that much interest in them, or don't have the time to do them. The medical director will certainly help solve these problems.

The following are some good reasons to set up the position:

■ Serve as liaison between the various systems inside and outside the organization. Internally, he or she would be a connecting person between the medical staff and administration. Externally, he or she could represent the organization to payer or provider organizations as appropriate, employers, patient groups, etc.

■ Recruit physicians. Having been recruited as a practicing clinician at an earlier time, he or she knows the questions and concerns a physician would have better than a lay person would.

■ Evaluate physician performance. This is best done by a peer.

■ Direct utilization review and quality assurance. Even though this function is done by many nurses, they have to be backed up by a physician executive in order to get cooperation from clinicians.

■ Assist CEO in helping physicians to understand the "big picture" and to become involved in strategic planning. Many physicians just see what is going on between them and their patients, and organizational needs can best be explained by someone who has worked at the bedside and also works in the administrative suite.

■ Develop clinical guidelines and outcomes management program. These guidelines and programs should be physician driven. A fellow physician can best help each clinical department to do that.

■ Be responsible for medical cost containment and allocation of resources. This is best done by a person who has a foot in both camps.

It's also important to be sure that there is general buy-in from the various critical parts of the organization:

■ In a hospital, by the administration and at least the leaders of the medical staff, if not the whole medical staff.

■ By individuals in the organization whose power might be impinged upon or changed by having a medical director—for instance, the elected president of medical staff and the vice president for clinical services in the administrative group or the elected president of the board of directors in a group practice. Also, the department chairs who report to the president of the medical staff might report to the medical director if the position is established.

■ By people lower in the chain of command, such as director of medical records or director of quality assurance, because these people would be reporting to one person in the old set up and might be reporting to the medical director in the new set up.

Write List of Responsibilities

Once you have dealt with the needs of the position and have gotten general buy-in, it is appropriate to develop a general list of responsibilities. At this point, it is not important to have a detailed job description. That can come later. It might be appropriate for the first person in the position to develop that with you. The general responsibilities would be different in each of the three sectors—groups, hospitals, and managed care organizations—as indicated in chapter 1.

Establish Reporting Lines

It is important for everyone, including the candidate for the position, to understand early in the planning process to whom the medical director will report. The medical director or the most senior physician executive must report directly to the chief executive officer or the board. Later, determine who will report to the medical director. The issue of authority must be dealt with early in the planning process. Ideally, authority should be somewhat equal to responsibility. If the position has a lot of responsibility but very little authority, the new medical director will be very frustrated and will probably receive very little respect from the medical staff or from administration.

Decide whether this is to be a line or a staff position. A line position means that the medical director not only has direct upward reporting lines but also downward and, to some extent, lateral lines (lateral reporting would be to other hospital vice presidents). He or she usually has some responsibility for profits and losses of the organization. In a staff position, the medical director is "a clinical resource for others in the organization, but...he or she...is not directly responsible for managing a department or adding specific value to the bottom line."[9]

In any of the three sectors, the position can work well either way, but it is very important to clarify which way the organization wants it to be.

Determine Salary

Candidates who apply for the job will want to know the salary range; a specific list of benefits to go with the base salary; whether there will be a bonus; and, if so, what percentage of the base salary the bonus will be. A number of organizations conduct regular compensation surveys in this area.[10-12] Their data can be invaluable in establishing compensation parameters for the position. If you are interviewing sophisticated and experienced candidates, they will be more impressed with the organization if all those financial issues have been dealt with prior to the interview. As an aside, it would be wise for the organization to have given thought to some kind of severance agreement or golden parachute. Again, the more experienced candidates will ask for this and will be impressed if you have already given it some thought. Along with salary issues, the organization should think early about a performance evaluation system and about how annual raises will be related to the results of performance evaluation.

Hire a Consultant

It is worth every penny the organization will spend to get help from a recruiting firm or an outside consultant as you develop this position. The American College of Physician Executives can direct you to experienced physician executive consultants who can help your organization, whether it is a hospital, a group practice, or a managed care organization.

The recruiting firm or the consultant should first ask all the interested parties what they want and then give them some advice about whether they want the right things. He or she can guide your organization in determining the responsibility and the comparable authority the medical director will have. The physician consultants will also tell how they do it in their organizations and how other organizations they have consulted with do it. You don't have to reinvent the wheel. Sometimes, consultants help with the recruitment and selection process. They also might help with orientation and on-the-job training. The consultant can help the organization develop a job description and reporting roles and can give advice regarding appropriate compensation packages.

Setting up Position/Selection and Recruitment Process

Group Practice

If the group has never had a formal medical director position, strong supporters of the concept should gradually but steadily broach this subject with the medical staff. Various parties, including many physicians and possibly administrators, will feel threatened at the prospect of establishing the position. Physicians will be concerned mostly about having a boss. Administrators will be concerned about having their management territory invaded. Both groups will have all sorts of prejudices about the position, based on whatever positive or negative things they have heard from colleagues around the country. As mentioned above, one way that negative biases can be dealt with is for the organization to have some outside consultants and medical directors, especially from similar sized groups, come and talk to the board of directors and the staff about the concept and about how the position functions in other organizations. It is also helpful to have some of the leaders of the organization attend national meetings where this subject is discussed regularly, such as the American Medical Group Association, the Medical Group Management Association, and the American College of Physician Executives.

Distribute to the physicians articles and other printed materials that help convince them of the need for the position. Such material is frequently available in *Physician Executive,* the journal of the American College of Physician Executives and in some of the books that the College publishes. The problems listed in the following quote would probably strike a cord of recognition with physicians, and they may be amenable to considering that a medical director could help solve some of the problems: "The health care industry is currently undergoing tremendous change due to increased competition, changing government policies, and consumer demands, and those multispecialty medical group practices with physician managers on their administrative teams will have a potentially greater degree of success in managing the turbulent years ahead."[13] Even though this statement was made in 1984, it still describes the current health care situation.

Early in the setting up process, it might be advisable for the board of directors to appoint a small ad hoc committee to do fact finding and to coordinate the information-gathering process. Topics the committee would research might be:

■ What do physician executives do?

■ How are they compensated?

■ What authority do they have?

It would be appropriate to give the committee a modest budget to work with and to make it clear to the medical staff that this committee is responsible for gathering information and has the eventual responsibility of making a recommendation to the board of directors and the staff. Any of the above-mentioned national organizations can help the committee by providing information, by sending in visiting consultants, and simply by reminding the committee to touch all of the necessary bases.

The ad hoc committee would look at areas and problems in the group that have not been properly dealt with by the administrative staff and by the elected or volunteer leadership of the group. Some of the common areas might be:

■ Evaluation of physician performance, including dealing with significant physician problems, such as impairment.

■ Liaison with other medical organizations in the community, with consumers, and with any other systems that affect the business of the group.

Usually, full-time clinicians have little interest in these functions or, if they do, have little time for them. If much liaison work is being done, it is usually by nonphysician administrators.

The committee might recognize that it is very important to have a physician who knows as much about the day-to-day functioning and business of the organization as the administrators do. Again, the elected president of the group and other elected full-time clinicians do not have time to get involved and probably should not be involved in day-to-day management anyway because of a lack of time. Management is not something you should do a little bit.

Especially in a group practice, it is important for this committee and other interested parties to gather information and look at the whole situation objectively, without having a certain person in mind for the job. When the committee is satisfied that the staff and the board of directors have reasonable information and exposure to the concept, they should be able to make a recommendation, such as: "We recommend that the group employ a physician executive who will spend x percent of his or her time in management and administrative functions and will receive compensation for those duties." Many of these positions start with the physician executive doing 50 percent clinical and 50 percent administrative, but we hear numerous stories of how they change to at least 75 percent administrative within a year. In the larger organizations many people say the position has to be 100 percent administrative to be effective.

The statement should also include a recommendation about reporting lines, general responsibilities, authority, and term of the appointment. Any of those factors may be changed once a specific person has been selected and is in place.

Once the recommendation has been made to the board and the staff and there is general acceptance and approval, the selection and recruitment process should begin immediately. First, recognize any interested internal candidates and make a decision about whether outside recruitment will be done. There are pros and cons about having the first medical director come from inside the organization versus outside. If the first medical director in a group practice comes from inside, everyone is familiar with the candidate. However, if the physician is chosen just because he or she is popular, that person will be doomed to early failure. It is important to identify someone who not only is popular and acceptable to the group but also has significant interest in and talent for day-to-day management.

If there are no realistic internal candidates, it will be necessary to do an outside search. It may be easier to identify someone from outside who has a proven track record and is a professional manager; however, everyone must recognize that it will take some time for that person to become accustomed to the new culture and environment. In some cases, that never happens. The issue of fitting in is so important that it deserves formal attention. One administrator and one or more physicians should be given the responsibility of seeing that the new physician executive from the outside is quickly incorporated into the culture.

Managed Care Organizations

Choosing a medical director for a managed care organization is a very different process from that of choosing one for a group practice or hospital, because physicians would have no say in the matter. The selection would probably be made in most cases by a national organization, an insurance company, or whatever organization ran the managed care organization. Large national and regional managed care organizations have medical director positions open all the time. Recruiters and management people in these organizations want someone with prior managed care experience who has a track record in utilization review, quality assurance, and professional relations.

Managed care organizations need to decide if they want someone who is a stronger "inside" person or has greater "outside" strengths. A strong inside person is usually someone with greater technical strengths, including experience in utilization review and quality assurance, computer knowledge, possibly budgeting experience, and an interest in tasks such as writing and developing policies.

An outside person usually has stronger oral communication skills. He or she is good at public relations, enjoys dealing with physicians and other health care providers face to face, and is willing to do public speaking and make sales presentations. It is not too common to find someone who is very strong in both areas. Many people with inside strengths are uncomfortable making public presentations, and people with outside strengths are miserable sitting behind a desk all day writing policy manuals and reviewing computer printouts.

Some physicians are content to do the specific tasks delegated to them and to function in a staff role. Others, with strong leadership skills, are probably interested in being leaders of organizations and will be frustrated in the former role. On the other hand, a person who is comfortable with the inside role may not be comfortable if thrust into a leadership position or into a position in which he or she has to have line management responsibilities for various departments and all sorts of professional and administrative people.

This is not to say that some of the skills in each area cannot be learned. Certainly basic utilization review skills can be learned by any reasonably motivated physician, so it is not that important for the person to have heavy experience in that area. Usually, managed care organizations have nurses on the staff who are strong in these areas, and they can teach this information to a new medical director. Communication skills and public relations skills can also be improved upon by anyone. Nevertheless, it is important for the applicants and the organization to understand from the beginning where the person's strengths and comfort zones are.

If an organization has recently experienced considerable problems with information systems and proper utilization of the information gathered from that system, it may want a strong inside medical director. Another organization might have experienced significant credibility and image problems in the marketplace with physicians, hospitals, employers, and members. In this case, a medical director who has strong public relations and communication skills might be more desirable.

A recurring concern in recent years has been that managed care organizations have tended to be more comfortable hiring people who have a track record in managed care, whether that track record was good or bad. They have tended to recycle medical directors who, for various reasons, have been less than successful with one or more organizations. Managed care organizations should be encouraged to hire physician managers who may have less experience but who seem to have the basic skills or personality required by the job. If people are hired who were fresh and not burned out, the organizations could then wisely invest time and money to properly train them.

Local managed care organization medical director positions can be either full- or part-time, depending on the size of the organization and the scope of responsibilities that the medical director will have. It is important that any managed care organization, whether it is a national, regional, or local, offer competitive salary and benefits in order to attract a qualified medical director.

One physician organization that warrants special mention is an independent practice (or physician) association (IPA). This entity started in the '70s and grew in popularity in the '80s and '90s as an alternative to traditional group- or staff-model HMOs. This more loosely knit type of physician organization has definite advantages for physicians who are not in large multispecialty groups and usually offers more access points for primary and specialty care than a traditional multispecialty group. If the IPA is to be as effective in cost containment and quality assurance as well-run group- or staff-model HMOs, it must have strong physician management and the cooperation of the independent physicians in the IPA. Among other strengths, the effective medical director in an IPA must be well versed in all aspects of managed care and have ample influencing skills.

Hospitals

It is the opinion of many executives in the hospital sector that a hospital that has more than 250 beds should have at least a part-time paid physician executive on its staff. The role that hospital medical staffs play in the governance, management, long-range planning, and day-to-day affairs of the hospital is becoming more complex and involved. "...[M]edical staffs need assistance in monitoring the quality of patient care, including overseeing quality assurance, utilization review, peer review, and credentialing.[14] It is increasingly difficult for physicians on the medical staff who are in full-time practice to devote the time that is needed for voluntary, elected administrative positions. Many physicians who would have been capable elected leaders of medical staffs are declining these positions of responsibility because so much time is required and because such a strain is put on their practice time and their personal lives. Therefore, it makes sense to have a full- or part-time medical director in any hospital of sufficient size to fill the roles and duties that were discussed in chapter 1.

Usually, the administrative staff recognizes that certain responsibilities that can only be carried out by physicians are falling through the cracks. At the same time, current and recent leaders of the medical staff will bring pressure to bear on administration to set up such a position. When there is interest from the administrative side and from the leaders of the medical staff, it is time to establish the position.

Just as in the group practice situation, the planning (search) committee should identify any interested internal candidates. If there are some strong and interested internal candidates, it may not be necessary to do an outside search. If not, it will be necessary to do an outside search using a competent search firm. The committee needs to determine the current salaries and benefits being paid in the marketplace. Administration and the medical staff have to agree on the most important functions for the medical director. Ideally, the organization will decide what problems are not being tended to and will hire someone who is qualified to solve them.

In the previous decade, many types of provider systems were busy trying to offer a broader scope of services to patients, employers, and payer organizations under one umbrella. This effort led to the term "integrated delivery system." The term, at its best, means that medical care is integrated and coordinated from beginning to end, with the outcome ideally being higher quality medical care combined with the most satisfactory customer service for the best price. An integrated delivery system might include a general hospital, a skilled nursing facility, and some type physician organization, all working together and possibly under one corporate umbrella. Or it might consist of several hospitals and physician organizations either loosely or tightly bound together. The permutations on the integrated system model are quite extensive.

Chief Medical Officer

As systems have integrated and become more complex, the need for physician executives with broader management experience and education has increased. Thus there is a need for chief medical officers who understand the management of patient care in the inpatient setting, episodic outpatient care, and long-term and chronic care. In addition to creating a need for more senior type chief medical officers, the development of integrated delivery systems has also created a need for medical management specialists—a medical director whose primary focus is quality or medical informatics or outcomes management, for example.

General Considerations

It is the authors' opinion that interpersonal skills are most important in helping the physician executive to handle the many interfacing functions of the position—negotiations, public relations, conflict management, and confrontation of problem physicians. This person probably will also be responsible for developing policies and overseeing quality assurance and utilization review. In all these functions, there is a clear and ongoing need for well-honed "people" skills.

There are likely to be physicians already on the staff who will have strong technical skills in many of these areas. However, they may never have been challenged in a way that provides clues to their interpersonal skills. Worse, the adage of familiarity breeding contempt may keep inside candidates from success in the position. The decision to hire from the inside should be made with a firm grip on the potential disadvantages for these candidates. Of course, outside candidates should also be subjected to close scrutiny on this score.

Chapter Three

Giving Authority, Power, and Influence to Physician Executives

"If lines of authority are blurred, or if the medical director is unable to gain the respect of the medical staff because of personality conflicts or other factors unique to the hospital/medical staff relation prevailing at a specific hospital, tensions between the medical staff and the medical director may erupt which might undermine the effectiveness of the medical director as a liaison between the medical staff and the administration."[4]

One way to give the new medical director authority is to set up clear reporting lines. In a hospital, the vice president of medical affairs should report directly to the CEO. In a managed care organization, the medical director should report directly to the top executive in the local or the regional organization. In a group practice, the medical director should report directly to either the board of directors or the CEO or president of the organization. In other words, in each type of organization the medical director must be a part of the upper management team and thus be involved in all affairs of upper management, including strategic planning. It is also necessary to be sure that everyone knows who reports to the medical director. If he or she is in a staff position, that may be the secretary. If there are other department heads or managerial people who should report to the medical director, that must be made very clear in the beginning, especially if those people had been reporting to someone else before this new position was set up.

The power of the medical director can be established by giving him or her control of some financial decisions and disciplinary actions and by including him or her in important meetings. However power is achieved, the medical director and other people in the organization need to understand exactly what power the medical director has.

In many organizations, the physician executive has financial limits. He or she can authorize the purchase of some things up to a certain dollar amount. For example, the medical director might purchase a piece of medical equipment or authorize a continuing education trip for a staff person. Usually, the medical director would have as much as or more financial decision-making power than anyone else in the organization except his or her boss. That's one way in which power can be understood by other people, because we all do respect financial control.

Also, be as clear as possible about disciplinary power. In some situations, the medical director has final power. In others, there is a limit to his or her power, and a decision may be passed to another group, such as the board of directors or a disciplinary committee. For example, the medical director may have the power to fire people if they are not doing their jobs. The medical director usually has this authority in a line position, where it is clearly understood by everyone that the medical director is the boss of all the staff physicians. That is usually the situation in an staff-model managed care organization but not in a group practice or hospital. In a group practice, the medical director's disciplinary action is usually limited to restricting someone's medical privileges. In many cases, it is necessary to make it clear to people that, when the medical director acts in a disciplinary role, he or she is acting on behalf of whomever he or she reports to. For example, in a group practice, this power is delegated to the medical director by the board of directors.

A task not relished by physician executives is confronting physicians about clinical performance or interpersonal behavior problems, but that task may be one of the main reasons the medical director was hired.

In a disciplinary action, you could try the following process:

1. Present the facts to the problem person.

2. Remind him or her of the expected behavior of all physicians in the organization

3. Tell him or her clearly what behavior change you expect.

4. Agree with him or her that they will change the behavior by a certain date.

5. Explain the consequences if the behavior is not changed.

An example of a hospital disciplinary action may help in understanding the steps. If a physician is not performing a surgical procedure properly, the medical director would tell him or her to get some retraining. After further training, the physician could resume doing the procedure, with a colleague observing for a specified period to see that everything was being done properly. Full privileges would be restored when the skills were at an acceptable level.

Another way in which organizations can bestow proper authority and power to physician executives is to include them in all information-sharing and decision-making meetings that impinge on their ability to do their jobs. The medical director and his or her superior need to decide together which meetings he or she should attend. It may not be important to sit in on every marketing meeting or every budget meeting, but, if information is given out or if decisions are made that will affect the medical director's domain or ability to do the job, he or she should be there. For example, the medical director should attend a marketing meeting that involves decisions about promotion and advertising of new services offered by the physicians. If the organization advertises that patients will have no more than a 15-minute wait before they are called in to see the doctor, the physicians on the staff need to know that. The physician executive will be delivering the message to them. In another example, a group practice might determine that, in order to be competitive, the primary care and ob-gyn departments must have evening hours, although the medical and surgical departments may not need to. The medical director, as well as other physician leaders, needs to participate in that decision-making process. Physicians will only accept information about these kinds of changes from a physician executive, and, even from him or her, it will not be an easy conversation.

The medical director also needs to be at meetings in which decisions or policies are being made because he or she may need to convince nonphysicians that a proposed policy is not realistic. For example, it would not be realistic to have a five-minute wait time policy.

The medical director needs to hear from people on the organization staff, such as marketing people, patient advocates, and nurses, who are the most sensitive to patients' needs and desires. They might tell the medical director how important a short wait time is, and he or she would relay that information to physicians. Many conscientious physicians would still think the most important thing is the interaction between the patient and the doctor and that, if that was a high-quality, satisfactory experience, it didn't matter how long you had to wait. It does matter. The medical director will need to influence physicians to believe that waiting time is important.

Probably one of the best ways to render someone powerless is to cut them out of significant decision-making meetings; it becomes known by everyone in the organization very quickly when that happens.

The medical director's boss determines the degree of influence that the medical director has by making it clear to the medical staff that the medical director speaks for the boss and by supporting decisions that the medical director makes, even if they have to have arguments behind closed doors before decisions are reached. Very early in the medical director's employment, however, people in the organization, including his or her boss, need to get a reading on how good the medical director's influence skills are. Does he or she get results, and are the people whom he or she has influenced happy to do what he or she asks? If he or she gets results in the traditional clinician's way of telling people what to do, that may not work over and over again. For example, in a committee meeting that the medical director chairs, it might have been the norm that people straggled in late and left early, and the meeting left people frustrated. The medical director could address the problem early on and request that people be prepared to come on time and stay until the end of the hour and explain why that was important. Then if the behavior started changing, people would be very impressed with the medical director's influence skills.

Physicians can improve their influence skills by improving all their communication skills, whether they involve public speaking, writing, listening, or personal appearance and grooming. All those things have a great deal of effect on one's power to influence. If you enunciate, speak at a moderate speed, and have a generally pleasant and confident tone of voice, people will want to do what you ask. If you write short memos with clear statements of what you want people to do, they will act quickly and not put your documents in a pile, thinking they'll read them when they have more time. If you write short e-mails that never take up more than one screen, people are more likely to read them. If you are a good listener, you will know what problems are brewing in your organization and move quickly to solve them rather than being surprised when some issue blows up. Many organizations and colleges offer courses on how to improve these skills.

Personal appearance and grooming are important. Not everyone was born beautiful, but everyone can smell good, look neat, and wear attractive, well-kept clothes appropriate to the organization's culture. Being well groomed is an important part of your ability to influence—people either want to be in your presence or they want to get away from you.

When a physician executive does not have the authority to get the job done, he or she is just not taken seriously by other people in the organization either above, lateral to, or below them. Their negotiating ability will be reduced within the organization. Their ability to discipline will be lessened, as will their ability to affect any kind of meaningful change. It's embarrassing to be in this position and not be able to get anything done. Medical directors in these situations are usually already looking for another job, but, if not, the search should definitely begin.

The following is an example of a medical director who once had the authority he needed, but lost it when his organization was bought by a new company:

"I was in a lame duck position in an organization in which I was the corporate medical director during a period of transition when a new owner was taking over from an old owner. I understood that I was only going to be in that position for 60 days. During the last 30 days of that transition period, the new president was trying to get new contracts negotiated with the staff physicians, and he wanted me to do those. I did do some of them, but, as time went on, I realized I didn't have much negotiating power because I knew and everyone else knew I was going to be leaving in a few weeks. So, for the last several weeks I was there, I didn't do any more contract negotiations, because there were some critical issues that needed to be dealt with by someone who was going to have ongoing power and influence. Physicians needed to negotiate money, benefits, and free time. If I negotiated with someone to work less on the weekends, and I was leaving, he or she wouldn't trust that it was actually going to happen."[15]

Another physician had a good salary and good working hours and seemed to have a fairly secure position, but he was not invited to important meetings, decisions were made that affected the doctors without his input, and the CEO was generally cool to him. The organization wanted a physician as a figurehead leader, but it did not want him to do much. He eventually changed jobs because he did not feel useful and influential.

Chapter Four

How To Convince a Medical Staff that Feels Threatened by the Idea of Having a Physician Executive that It Needs One

As in any other convincing or selling job, the first thing that people in favor of the position have to do is try their best to understand why the staff is threatened. It is much easier to respond to threats and fears if you know exactly where they are coming from and what they are related to. Physicians may fear that they will have a boss, that more power may shift to the administrative camp, that regulation will increase, or that they will lose influence because they give up doing some tasks. Sometimes we've been so convinced of the need for the position that we've tried to pressure the opposing side into it with all sorts of logic. That doesn't ever seem to work. It is better salesmanship to let people convince themselves of the need for something. If you listen carefully to the skeptics and then respond, you are more likely to finally convince them.

In staff-model managed care organizations, it is just a given to have a medical director. In IPA models, physicians who contract with the managed care organization as members of the IPA welcome having a medical director as an interface for them with the insurance executives. In hospitals and group practices, probably the biggest fear that physicians have rises from the fact that they do not like the idea of having a boss. They try to label their concern more rationally, so they call it a concern over additional overhead and lost dollar productivity. In response to that fear in a group practice setting, it is probably best for the first medical director not to be a boss. He or she can be in a position that reports directly to the board of directors, to the president, or to the highest authority in the organization. Over time, the medical director position may develop into a boss situation and the staff can adjust to it, but, in the beginning, it's probably not a good idea.

"Many physicians and medical staffs believe that the medical director wants to control them, but that simply isn't true. The medical director's job is to lead, to provide continuity, and to help the organization achieve what it said it wanted to do....the medical director is the most up to date member of the medical staff on administrative, legal, legislative, and reimbursement issues. The medical director is there when the medical staff needs someone to lend a sympathetic ear. The medical director understands the total problems of physicians better than the nonphysician CEO."[16]

In the hospital setting, the medical director or vice president for medical affairs is usually not the boss of any physicians unless he or she is in a hospital large enough that he or she has some other management physicians under him or her. In this case, we wouldn't be talking about setting up a position; we'd be talking about a position that had been long developed. One other scenario in which the VPMA might be a boss of other physicians would be if salaried clinicians—such as pathologists, emergency department physicians, etc.—report directly to him or her.

One good way to sell the concept of a medical director to a fearful medical staff is to have them do some brainstorming about some basic questions:

- How would you like for things to be different in the hospital or group practice?

- What would you like to have more of?

- What would you like to have less of?

When they come up with their list for these questions, it may be possible to show them how having a medical director would enhance the likelihood of achieving their goals. For example, they might say they would like to have an effective quality assurance program. Most organizations have reasonably good ways of monitoring or assessing quality but not necessarily good ways of ensuring that the level of quality improves. It might be that the medical director who concentrated on these quality issues could help the staff to ensure improvement. He or she has the time to drive the quality assurance system—remind people of what they are supposed to do, praise them for doing it, get some jobs done for them. For example, a staff physician might have the responsibility to review a large number of charts, and the medical director might be able to help the physician get that done by suggesting that a clerical person or a medical records librarian could actually do almost all the review, saving just a few highlights for the doctor to review. As a result, the job could be done quicker, with less of the physician's time involved.

In a hospital setting, the medical staff might say that it wished that administration understood its side of issues better, and the administration might say it wished that doctors understood the costs of running the hospital better. An effective medical director could help in a liaison role. For example, administration could think it would be cost effective and efficient to keep operating rooms open for scheduled surgery on Saturdays and Sundays. You can expect that there would be resistance from surgeons. The driving force behind administration's view would be to provide more services and to gain a competitive edge on other hospitals in the community. If people could have scheduled surgery done on a Saturday, they would reduce the number of days they missed from work. Ideally, the medical director would be able to explain the issues to the surgeons, reminding them that service to customers is what will keep the hospital in business. From the other side of the equation, surgeons may ask the medical director to explain to administration that some new equipment is needed or that a surgical physician assistant should be hired for the hospital.

In the brainstorming session, someone might state that the organization needs a better way of dealing with physicians who have interpersonal communication problems. The medical director can be the one who confronts these physicians and says, "You must change this behavior or you will lose something (your job, a promotion, or a bonus). I want you to get some kind of counseling."

If hospital leaders know of another hospital in a nearby community with a medical director, they might ask someone from the hospital to speak to the medical staff, if it's not a direct competition situation. Otherwise, they could ask the American College of Physician Executives for a referral, saying, "We are considering developing the position of vice president of medical affairs, and we would like to have someone from a similar size hospital come talk to our executive committee and medical staff about the value of the position." The elected president of the other hospital's medical staff could come and make the presentation. You would pay his or her travel expenses and a modest stipend. The speaker should be briefed ahead of time about the hospital's history, its power structure, and the current relationship between administration and physicians so that he or she can tailor the talk to meet your particular needs.

Most organizations are glad they have medical directors. The people who are involved in running the organization at the board level or at some other significant committee level appreciate it. It's not realistic to expect that much of the rank and file will appreciate it. In a hospital setting, it doesn't cost the doctors any money, so, once the position is in place and the person is doing an acceptable job, the rank and file physicians don't care, because they don't really notice that much. They usually have concerns before the position is filled or during the early months of the person's tenure when they still don't know what the person is doing and they are worried that he is going to boss them around too much.

In a group practice setting, doctors may not see much value in the position, even after the person has been doing a good job for a few years. In this setting, you just hope they don't see too much negative about the position—cost or otherwise. People will eventually get used to the cost of the position, just as they get used to the cost of bigger house payments or higher taxes.

I don't think we should ever expect that new management positions will be approved by everyone. Realistically, we have to expect that the people who are heavily involved in the organization will approve of it or will become sold on it after the fact, that the minority of dissidents will be very small and can be dealt with, and that the majority really won't care very much. Some of the majority will accede to the people who they believe are in power or who know more about the inner workings of the organization. Anyone who has had freedom in a certain area is going to resist giving some of it up. That's just human nature. People need time to think about what they might get and what they would be willing to give up in any new deal.

Physicians fear losing freedom if they have a medical director. They think: "This person will be looking over my shoulder more than I am accustomed to, will create more of a bureaucracy that will place more demands on my free time. He or she will be a pawn of the administration and not really a physician anymore."

The gains can be greater than the losses. Outside sources have already taken many freedoms from physicians. The medical director can help the physicians cope and flourish in a changing health care environment. The clinicians will have an advocate who is one of them, explaining their positions and needs to administration. They will have somebody on the administrative staff who is knowledgeable and has the time to help the doctors do the things they need to do in the areas of quality assurance, credentialing, marketing services, and keeping up with government regulations.

Chapter Five

What You Have to Do to Become a Physician Executive

Become a board-certified clinician who practices for at least 3-5 years.

Residents who are interested in management and who do not want to practice clinically have asked, "Why do I need to be board certified when I am not going to practice?" As a medical director you will be working with physicians—in some cases, telling them what they can and cannot do. Physicians respect other physicians most for their knowledge of disease and for their capacity to take care of patients. Only gradually do they come to respect them for their management skills. They will not take instructions from someone who has not had to cope with an overcrowded schedule, shrinking resources, government regulations, the threat of malpractice suits, and night call, to name a few of the frustrating realities of being a practicing clinician.

"Physician [executives] should be experts in dealing with other physicians, defining appropriate clinical practices, establishing quality controls....[T]hey should also have developed an appreciation for work in the trenches; demonstrated the ability to relate to patients and peers; and, in general, attained a position of credibility among a wide range of colleagues."[17]

The aspiring medical director does not have to practice full time, but the practice has to be in a setting in which you are fully responsible for some patients. Nancy Ashbach, MD, MBA, says, "The clinical experience is critical—five years of it but not necessarily full time. Urgent care facilities where you haven't had full responsibility for patients are not as good as half time for Kaiser or half time for a group."[18]

Get management experience.

Serve on and lead committees and task forces. These are activities that are good for gaining management experience:

- Quality assurance committee.

- Environmental scanning committee, which tries to be aware of what changes are going on in the health care field at large.

- Legislative action committee, which addresses activities affecting health care in the state legislature and in Congress.

■ Committee that deals with censoring members of the medical society and responding to complaints regarding those physicians. If a patient feels wronged by a physician, the board of censors would confront that physician about alleged actions, get both sides of the story, and then come up with some resolution.

Let people see you doing management activities—working with people and tackling problems. If you lead the long-range planning committee, the utilization review and quality improvement committee, or the credentialing committee, you can claim all of them as experience when you are ready to move more directly into management.

Some other ways to get experience are: Get involved in the county medical society, the state medical society, or the American Medical Association. You can also get management experience by "...participating in American Academy of Pediatrics in chapter, committees, and sections, directing or managing your office or division, serving on hospital committees, or holding a leadership position with an IPA, PHO, or managed care organization. These experiences will help provide you with a more complete picture of the executive without making a commitment and will serve you well when you are job-hunting.[19]

Some managed care organizations and insurance companies hire people to do utilization review and quality assurance part time. Your hospital may need a physician to do some part-time management. If you could get away from your practice for one or two half days a week to do some part-time management tasks in your hospital, this would also be a valuable source of experience.

If you think you might be interested in hospital management, you would be wise to do what you can to move up in the elected or appointed hierarchy of the hospital medical staff. Express interest in becoming chair of your clinical department or be willing to serve on the hospital executive committee. Be available to take a job as an elected officer of the hospital staff. The same would be true for those aspiring to positions in management in group practices or in various types of managed care organizations.

Many men and women go into management in the middle of their careers. They may reach the point where they feel they have done all the cardiovascular surgery they want to do or they can't discuss otitis media one more time. It is no longer a challenge; they need a new challenge. Many people come to the point in their careers that they want or need a change. Volunteer for committees throughout your career to continually learn new activities, to make yourself visible in the organization, and to gain experience to put on your resume should you decide some day that management appeals to you.

Be prepared to move.

You may have to take a management job that is not quite right in order to get the necessary experience. Once you go into the management arena, you may have to move every 3-5 years. "...[T]urnover is particularly high among medical directors in managed care organizations, where, according to several human resource directors interviewed, the average tenure is approximately 18 months."[20] You need to think about whether you and your family are prepared to move often. Some couples think moving is invigorating and a great new challenge. Others, especially the spouse of the physician executive, had planned to live their entire lives in the city where the physician set up practice. Recruiters frequently say the unwillingness to move is the greatest barrier for a physician who wants to move into management.

Get education.

The Physician in Management seminars of the American College of Physician Executives are an excellent source of training in basic management skills. Attend various specific management courses offered by ACPE that fill in management knowledge gaps that you may have identified. Be on the alert for informal educational opportunities from other national professional organizations and from local colleges and universities. Get a master's degree in management if you have the time and the financial resources. Increasingly, employers will consider those who have master's degrees above those who don't if two candidates have an equal amount of management experience. "An MBA or similar degree was important fifteen years ago, but now most recruiters insist on it, especially for the full-time positions."[19]

Be aware, however, that a master's degree will help you do a management job, but it will not guarantee that you can get a management job the way the MD or DO guaranteed that you could go some place and practice clinically. You will still need experience to get the management job.

D. H. Cordes, MD, claims, "To become effective managers, physicians must gain proficiency in seven skill areas: computer applications, budgeting, fiscal control, political or regulatory process, personnel management, program development, and planning and organization."[21] Physician managers also need to speak well, listen carefully, run effective meetings, make presentations, and write clearly. You can take courses that will teach you how to do these things.

Find a mentor.

Roger Schenke, ACPE Executive Vice President, advises: "Find yourself a mentor—male or female. Someone who has experience who will help you think. Look for someone who is an effective person. If you admire the person and think you would like to be more like him or her, try to get on a committee that the person is on, or in an educational program that the person is in. Get in the same room, get to know the person. It will be natural for the conversation to be around management issues. Then ask: 'How does someone get involved in management in this organization? How did you get to where you are? Has this management change been good for you? What education did you get?' If that person sees you begin to do management activities, he or she becomes like your mother or father, because he or she helped to get you started."[22]

Mentoring takes less time than many people think. The person does not have to be in your organization or even in your town. You can call them and say, "Can you listen to me for a while? 20-30 minutes."

Mentoring does not have to be regular. I have heard people try to set up formal situations—a contract where I'll help you with your weaknesses and you help me with mine. Once in a while that might work, but a formal commitment to a specific amount of time can scare people off. They may give you that much time because they get interested in you, but they don't want to promise it.

In some companies, mentor situations exist in which someone spends a considerable amount of time at another site of that company—at another hospital in the same hospital system or at another staff model in the same managed care system. A new medical director can be sent to the site and walk around with an experienced medical director for a week and learn how he or she does things. CIGNA, Kaiser Permanente Medical Groups, and some of the Catholic hospital systems train new medical directors in this way.

Information interviews are valuable and may be the beginning of a mentoring relationship. There are two types. First, you can have an information interview with a physician in management who has a job that you think you would like. For instance, if you are interested in group practice management, interview several physicians who are physician executives in group practices. These information interviews may lead to a long-term mentor relationship.

A second type of information interview would be one in which you interview someone who works for an organization for which you might like to work. If you desire an information interview with a health care executive in a large insurance company, plan two or three questions that you would ask that person and tell them ahead of time that you do not intend to take more than 15 minutes of their time. You should have the key questions written out so you could at least get them answered if there is not time to get other questions dealt with. Of course, if you already know the person, it would be all right to expect a longer interview or possibly an interview over lunch that you pay for.

Use your network contacts. If you want an information interview with a vice president of medical affairs, ask someone who knows him or her to set up the interview. Your friend might call a VPMA in Atlanta and say, "John would like to come and talk with you for 15 minutes about what your job is like because he is interested in going into that kind of work." Your network contact would be a little like the matchmaker in "Fiddler on the Roof" who arranged marriages.

You could also make that call yourself, but it would be nice if you had a name to drop and could say, "George Linney suggested that I call you. I'm going to be in Atlanta on business next week, and I was wondering if I could have 15 minutes of your time to ask you a few questions about your work?"

ACPE's Physician Executive Advisory Service (PEAS) can connect you with an experienced physician executive who will tell you how he or she moved into medical management or moved into a more senior physician executive position. Available to ACPE members only, the PEAS program, allows you to ask for advice on a career issue or for guidance about a specific work-related project or task. You can be connected by calling or e-mailing the College and letting them know what your needs are.

Mentoring relationships are valuable. Take care of them. Say thank you verbally or in a written thank-you note when you receive help. Be cautious about your behavior. Don't continue a mentoring relationship if sexual stuff gets in the way. It is very natural for people who work together to become good friends. The sparks of creativity generated by good minds thinking together can sometimes lead to sexual thoughts. If either person acts on these thoughts, it is wise to end a mentoring relationship. The trouble you can get into can outweigh any benefits you might receive from the relationship.

Leland Kaiser, PhD, says "...[W]e are all mentors for the people who have not moved as far on the path as we have, and at the same time we are dependent on mentors who are further along on the journey to help us take the next step....You may never be able to help the people who help you. Your service is to those who are coming along behind you."[23]

Improve interpersonal communication skills.

One CEO has said, "My present position as CEO is dependent on constant attention to the development of interpersonal skills, including patience, tolerance for delays, comfort with ambiguity, and learning to negotiate win-win situations. Never before were listening and communication skills more important."[24]

"...[T]he position of manager demands that an individual be able to develop networks of relationships which depend almost entirely on the art of communication."[25]

If you are aspiring to an executive position where you will be expected to deal with the public and represent your organization in all sorts of public situations, you must become an effective speaker. Do not assume that you are an effective speaker just because you have had a lot of education or because you have had experience making scientific presentations at medical meetings. Most physicians will testify that the speeches given at their specialty society meetings are dull lectures that are read. It would be a good idea for you to have an experienced person critique your public speaking style the next time you make a speech or, even better, to work on this skill with a trainer using video equipment.

Also, if you want a job where you will be in line management and directly responsible for people, get some training in performance evaluation. Performance evaluations in health care organizations are generally not done well; none of us is born knowing how to give appropriate criticism and constructive feedback. You need to speak clearly and concisely in a calm, firm voice when giving people feedback about changes they need to make in their behavior. If you look all around the room or fidget nervously, you convey uncertainty and fear. You want to appear confident. If this is difficult for you, practice in front of a video camera until you improve.

Take courses, read books, practice whatever you think your weaknesses are. "I thought I could speak well and listen well, but I knew I avoided necessary confrontation with some men. It was not necessary for me to become someone who screamed and confronted everyone on everything I didn't like. It was necessary for me to calmly and clearly say what I wanted in some situations without retreating, brooding, and never saying what I thought and felt. I've worked on that for years. I'm much better."[26]

Spend time on your resume.

Put together a short(no more than 3 pages), powerful resume, as opposed to a long curriculum vitae, which most physicians have. You not only tell where you showed up for work and when (the items usually included in the CV), but also what you accomplished while you were there. List your professional experience in reverse chronological order. People want to know most what you have been doing in the past 3-5 years, even though they want to read about all of your experience. To keep the resume to 3 pages or less, you can abbreviate activities that occurred 5 years or more ago.

When you choose items from your curriculum vitae, most likely you will have to add information. True, you worked at St Vincent's Hospital from 1996 to 2000, but what did you do while you were there? Did you help lower costs in the emergency department? Tell how much was saved. If you worked for a managed care facility, you might say: "Developed four new satellite offices, recruited eight primary care physicians over a two-year period, and reduced the length of stay from 300 to 200 days per 1,000, which resulted in a first-time operational surplus for the plan."

Notice the numbers. People like to know that you have saved an organization money or increased its revenues, and they want to know how much and over what period. Use numbers to prove your general statements whenever you can.

Use networking effectively.

Get to know more people than you know now. Most people get jobs because they know someone who knows someone that led to the position. People have to know who you are and what you can do in order to recommend you for a job. They need to see you tackling problems, working with people, managing people and information. We've known a few people who didn't have all the experience that the company wished that they had, but someone knew them and thought they had the qualities it would take to do the job.

How do you network? Increase your visibility—make speeches, write articles, lead committees. Make phone calls, attend meetings and talk to people while you are there, send letters, send thank you notes, call people again, read journals for advertised positions. Review Web sites that have job postings. It's more work than most people want to do, but few people get to skip it.

Contact search firms. Get to know the professional recruiters in several search firms that deal regularly with the sectors of the health care industry of interest to you. Many of the most reputable executive recruitment firms, particularly those with well-developed physician executive practices, have regular ads in the classified section of the *Physician Executive Journal* and on the ACPE Web site. Professional recruiters are excellent networkers. They may be able to help you find the job you want at no cost to you as well as help you expand your network.

Hone your interviewing skills.

Research the position before you arrive for the interview. Talk to people in the organization if possible. A reputable recruiter will provide you with a job description and tell you about the organization and the city in which it is located. "Don't even interview for jobs that have no written descriptions, budgets, and goals. You'd think everyone would know this by now, but, in the heat of the moment, people do buy the 'we'll work things out' story."[27]

Here is a list of questions that people have often been asked in interviews. The best technique to become prepared and relaxed before the interview is to write out the answers to the questions first and then practice speaking them in front of a video camera. It is nice to have a friend or spouse pretend to be the interviewer, but it is also effective to practice by yourself and then watch the tape.

- Tell me briefly what you've been doing since medical school.
- Why are you looking for a job?
- Why did you leave your last job?
- What were you major responsibilities in your last job?
- What is your greatest strength and your greatest weakness? (Try to couch the weakness in a positive light. Example: I've been told that sometimes I'm too compassionate with subordinates.)
- What are your long- and short-term goals? Example of long-term goal: Become CEO of a health care organization. Short term: Develop expertise in utilization management.
- What are your three greatest accomplishments in your career? Example: Led organization as it changed from being a local health care provider to a regional provider.

■ What kind of contribution can you make to our company? Example: I believe I can organize and energize the medical staff so that it members will feel more supportive of the goals of the company.

■ How do you react to criticism?

■ Describe a time when you made a big mistake and how you handled it.

■ Can you give me an example of how you have managed people in the past?

■ How will your spouse feel about your taking this job, about relocating, about your work-related travel?

■ Have you ever hired or fired someone? Explain your process.

■ Why do you want a career in management?

■ How would you deal with a physician who is not performing well?

■ Describe your experience with utilization review and quality assurance.

■ How might you bridge the communication gap between physicians and administrators?

■ Describe a time when you analyzed a problem, set a goal, created strategies for solving the problem, implemented the plan, and evaluated the results?

You need good, thoughtful answers to these questions, but you also need to pay close attention to how you look and sound when you are answering them. Do you sound confident but not arrogant or argumentative? Do you sit up straight, walk holding yourself up—not slouched over looking meek. Do you have a firm handshake, but not one that breaks knuckles? Do your clothes fit well; do you look businesslike, conservative? For women, tailored suits and dresses with nothing low-cut at the neck and no extremely short skirts. For men, dark suits with ties that are not overly flashy.

Physicians will generally have two distinct thoughts when considering a move into medical management: "...[A]m I doing this because of a positive motivation or because of dissatisfaction with my present situation? Most physicians move into administration because of a motivation for the change....Many wish to take a leadership role in dealing with the ever-present changes around us. Some look at a desire for professional growth. Others genuinely feel that they can make an impact on health care at a higher level than in their offices. A smaller number choose to change because of a dissatisfaction element. Competition may be forcing practices to contract or to be unpleasant. Some may feel stale and tired of doing the same thing every day. Some may feel unable to keep up with the changes in practice and the limitations imposed by third parties. Others may be attracted to the concept of more regular hours with no call."[19] Whatever your reasons, it is important to declare positive motives by the time you get ready for an interview.

Plan on several interviews.

Certainly, physicians who are getting ready to change from clinical careers to full-time management should interview for several positions before deciding on the right job, especially if they are going to have to make a geographic move. If a health care organization thinks enough of you to offer to pay your expenses to come for an initial interview, recruiters tell us that it is all right to go for that initial interview if you are more than 50 percent interested in the job. If you or your spouse is totally closed to living in that city or to working for that organization, it is not appropriate for you to interview for the position at the organization's expense. On the other hand, if you have doubts but are open to the possibility, it is perfectly all right to go for that initial interview.

Generally, health care organizations interview at least 3-5 candidates in the first round of interviews. Then, the organization or its search committee will have narrowed the list to one or two finalists, and, in that case, it will invite both finalists back for second interviews. Usually, the spouse is included in the second interview trip; a physician executive should never take a job and the organization should never make a formal offer unless the spouse has had a least one visit.

Experienced executive recruiters say that the three most important issues for a candidate to consider are:

■ How interesting and challenging is the position being offered?

■ Is the location appealing to me and my spouse and family?

■ Is the total compensation package attractive?

The answer to at least two of these questions should be strongly positive and the answer to the third question should be at least somewhat positive.

Be prepared for change.

■ Change in responsibilities and job description.

■ Change in reporting relationships and change in bosses.

■ Change in the way your compensation is figured. Many organizations are moving toward placing increasing amounts of executives' total compensation at risk based on individual and organizational performance.

■ Drastic changes in the marketplace in which you are working. There was a big move to integrate systems, and now some of them have begun to reverse the process. Organizations are merged, reengineered, downsized. The euphemisms continue to spring up, but all of them mean a volatile market in which it seems almost anything can happen. Whatever the mutations, organizations are going to need physician executives to lead them because only a physician already understands the clinical issues and can learn the needed management skills.

Summary

More and more hospitals, group practices, managed care organizations, and businesses are seeing the need for physicians in administrative positions in their organizations. Increasingly, clinicians who have practiced for a while become interested in the workings of the entire medical organization and want to influence the future direction of health care. The joining of these two desires is creating challenging opportunities for physicians interested in management. Both organizations and physicians can benefit from the active presence of physicians in management roles. The secret will be to design the positions carefully so that they respond to rigorously determined organizational needs, to enlist the support of both administration and the medical staff for the position, and to recruit as widely as possible to ensure the best fit of physician and position. For the physician interested in entering management, there can be no better guidance than that of a colleague who has already made the plunge.

References

1. Kindig, D. "The Changing Managerial Role of Physician Executives." *Journal of Health Administration Education* 7(1):34-46, Winter 1989.

2. Martin, W. "The Levers of Influence." *Physician Executive* 25(6):8-14, Nov.-Dec. 1999.

3. Riffer, J. "Hospitals Shift Toward Paid Medical Directors." *Hospitals* 60(4):98, Feb. 20, 1986.

4. "Role of the Medical Director." *HMSS Newsletter* 4(6):1-2, June 1987.

5. Coile, R. "Physician Executives in the 21st Century: New Realities, Roles, and Responsibilities." *Physician Executive* 25(5):8-13, Sept.-Oct. 1999.

6. Bujak, J. "Culture in Chaos: the Need for Leadership and Followership in Medicine." *Physician Executive* 25(3):17-24, May-June 1999.

7. Boruch, F. "We Can Be Heroes." *Physician Executive* 25(2):44-50, March-April 1999

8. Russell C. Coile Jr., CHI Systems Division, Superior Consultant Company, Inc., Plano, Tex., personal communication, September 2000.

9. Bloomberg, M. "Management Training for the Physician Executive." *Physician Executive* 18(2):10-4, March-April 1992.

10. *Physician Executive Compensation Survey, 1999.* St. Louis, Mo.: Cejka & Company, 1999.

11. *Physician Executive Compensation Report: The 2000 Survey of Chief Medical Officers.* Tampa, Fla.: Physician Executive Management Center, 2000.

12. *Executive Compensation Survey.* Oakbrook Terrace, Ill.: Witt/kieffer, Ford Hadelman and Lloyd, 2000.

13. Downes, R. "The Role of Physician Managers in Larger Multispecialty Groups." *College Review* 1(2):83-95, Autumn 1984.

14. Riffer, J. "Hospitals Shift toward Paid Medical Directors." *Hospitals* 60(4):98, Feb. 20, 1986.

15. Personal experience of the first author, George Linney, MD.

16. Cohn, R. "Hospital Management's Linchpin: The Medical Director." *Physician Executive* 14(2):18-20, March-April 1988.

17. Hartfield, J. "The Costs, Challenges, and Rewards of Management." *Physician Executive* 14(4):3-5, July-Aug. 1988.

18. Nancy Ashbach, MD, Network Medical Director, MetLife of Colorado, Denver, personal communication, 1992.

19. Wallace, P. "Negotiating Change: Making the Switch from Practice to Administration." *Newsletter of the Section on Administration and Practice Management,* American Academy of Pediatrics. 6(1):5, Spring 2000.

20. Hirsch, G. "Physician Career Management: Organizational Strategies for the 21st Century." *Physician Executive* 25(2):30-5, March-April 1999.

21. Cordes, D., and others. "Management Roles for Physicians: Training Residents for the Reality." *Journal of Occupational Medicine* 30(11):863-7, Nov. 1988.

22. Roger Schenke, Executive Vice President, American College of Physician Executives, Tampa, Fla., personal communication, 1992.

23. Kaiser, L. *Lifework Planning.* Brighton, Colo.: Brighton Books, 1989, p. 7.

24. Henry, R. "The Road to System CEO." In *Roads to Medical Management: Physician Executives' Career Decisions.* Tampa, Fla.: American College of Physician Executives, 1988, p. 39.

25. Gelmon, S., and Mickevicius, V. "Do Physicians Manage? A Perspective on Physician-Managers in Teaching Hospitals." *Health Management Forum* 5(4):55-65, Winter 1984.

26. Experience of the second author, Barbara Linney, MA.

27. Kennedy, M. "When to Counter and When Not." *Physician Executive* 25(3):67-9, May-June 1999.

Further Reading

Belton, G., and Baron, C. "Profile of the HMO Medical Director." *Medical Group Management Journal* 34(2):17-22, March-April 1987.

Bloom, D. "The Chief of Staff and the Medical Director." *Physician Executive* 16(1):21-2, Jan.-Feb. 1990.

Fine, A. "New Challenges for Medical Directors." *Physician Executive* 16(2):36-7, March-April 1990.

Hershey, N. "Documenting Roles and Responsibilities." *Physician Executive* 16(4):25-7, July-Aug. 1990.

Kirschman, D., and Grebenschikoff, J. *Physician Executive Guide: Everything You Need to Know about Creating and Filling a Physician Executive Position.* Tampa, Fla.: Physician Executive Management Center, 1990.

Lepinot, A. "Does Your Hospital Need a Full-Time Physician Manager?" *Trustee* 40(2):19-23, Feb. 1987.

Linney, B. *Hope for the Future, A Career Development Guide for Physician Executives.* Tampa, Fla.: American College of Physician Executives, 1996.

Matheson, G., and Gill, S. "Good Management for Good Medicine, The Role of the Vice President for Medical Affairs." *Healthcare Executive* 3(5):31-3, Sept.-Oct. 1988.

"Physician Execs Watch Salaries, Roles Expand." *Hospitals* 65(8):68,70, April 20, 1991.

Roberts, N., and Melnick, G. "The Evolving Role of the Medical Director." *Physician Executive* 15(3):18-21, May-June 1989.

Ruelas, E., and Leatt, P. "The Roles of Physician-Executives in Hospitals: A Framework for Management Education." *Journal of Health Administration Education* 3(2, Pt. 1):151-69, Spring 1985.

Rumsey, J. "Group Practices Need Medical Director as Go-Between." *American Medical News* 30(35):32, Sept. 18, 1987.

Sweeney, D. "Why Every Group Needs a Managing Doctor." *Medical Economics* 65(19):60-2,67, Oct. 3, 1988.